I Can Wonder Anything

poems

Terence Degnan

Finishing Line Press
Georgetown, Kentucky

I Can Wonder Anything

Copyright © 2023 by Terence Degnan
ISBN 979-8-88838-123-6 First Edition
All rights reserved under International and Pan-American Copyright Conventions. No part of this book may be reproduced in any manner whatsoever without written permission from the publisher, except in the case of brief quotations embodied in critical articles and reviews.

ACKNOWLEDGMENTS

Versions of these poems can be found in the following Publications/Journals:

The Blood Pudding, *There Is a Thin Knot*

Pittsburgh Poetry Journal, *Every Time I Pass the Room in Manhattan Where My Daughter Was Born*

Wild Roof Journal, *I Raise Her to be Free*

What Rough Beast, *I Have No Time for the Poets*

Poetry is Bread, *It's My Beach*

Love's Executive Order, *The Disc Jockey on the Radio*

High Shelf Press, *I Name This Scar My Brother*

Publisher: Leah Huete de Maines
Editor: Christen Kincaid
Cover Art: Travis Swain Pendlebury
Author Photo: Samuel Robinson

Order online: www.finishinglinepress.com
also available on amazon.com

Author inquiries and mail orders:
Finishing Line Press
P. O. Box 1626
Georgetown, Kentucky 40324
U. S. A.

Table of Contents

I. *The Wooden Boy From Rochysteria*
It's My Beach 1
Did You Move the Coffee Pot 3
My Soul is Unfortunately a Bird 5
Old Make of the Old Car 7
Hitchhiking to Cannan 11
In the Photo of You 13
I Never Thought of Myself as Much of a Gardener 15
On a Mattress We Couldn't Replace 20
Dear Wife, ... 21
I Would Like to Have Entered the Kitchen 23
Now is Always Escaping Me 24
Watching the Cryptographers 25
I Name This Scar My Brother 26
I Began to Wonder 29
I'm Old Enough 31
On Second Thought 33
The Devil and Robert Johnson 35
In the Dream Where You Were Me 37
There is a Thin Knot 38
Much Like Edith 39
Every Time I Pass the Room in Manhattan Where My
    Daughter Was Born 40
All of the Sudden 42
I Haven't Laughed Like That in Years 43
In the Dream You Said 44
What We Weren't Taught About the Middle 45
What I have Put in Place of Church 48
Try to Imagine Me 49
Schrödinger's Karl 51
My Father is Over There 53
The Weak Binary 55
I Wish 57
I Am Not the Man 58
I Would Like to Believe 59

II. *Concerning Midnight Gardeners*

She Waters the Cilantro ... 63
Being a Taxi Driver is Hard Work ... 65
What We'll Do ... 67
The Cat is Old ... 69
They Made Us Humans ... 72
When I Write the Older Gentleman Into the Poem ... 74
Sunset Park ... 75
On Not Seeing the Red Bird Off the Coast of Argentina ... 77
Vestiges ... 79
More Than Ever ... 81
It's Not the Shoe Polish ... 83
The Most Sacred Thing in Brooklyn ... 86
In Puerto Vallarta ... 87
I Raise Her to Be Free ... 88
It's Days Like These ... 90
The Matriarchy Draws a Line ... 92
The Alphabet Silo! ... 93
We Sat For Hours ... 94
Pathetic Fallacy ... 96
There's This Piano ... 97
You Have to Put the Spoon in Your Mouth ... 100
The Moon is From Montana ... 102
One of the Most Beautiful Things ... 104
I Have No Time For the Poets ... 105
Should You Meet Me on Your Way Home to Rochester ... 108

for Melanie & Lola

I. *The Wooden Boy From Rochysteria*

"If you ever need a skin for your drum, remember me."
—*Pinocchio*

It's My Beach

that's my skyline
you'd have to be
occupying my math
to dilute the anomaly
that is me

that's my breakup scene
for myriad reasons
that's my favorite bar

not to mention
my specific sum of heartbreaks
and broken-bone memories
swaying in the closet
with the skeletons
that make up my lore

see that kid
on the closed-circuit TV
kissing a girl named Hillary
up against
Josh's car
go and get your own
Hillary and Josh

hear that choppy jingle
from an old mattress commercial
in a shoddy dated mixtape
that's my mistake
that's my sum of butterflies
where, rotting in the attic
of my synapses
I'm still halfway across the monkey bars
chasing my shadow
in a Catholic School uniform

to be fair, I can't be 100% positive
that the sundials in our memories
obey modern orbits
it could be chasing me

your Rochester
isn't my hometown
even if we did
share the same crib
we don't have the same combinations
you can borrow my bike
all you like
but you'd have to adjust the aperture
to occupy my glee
and the whole time
you'd be wearing me
you can *Rochester* all you want
but you'll be defending a backwards flag
when my bully comes through
and knocks the ghost out of you

for all I know
my paper tigers
could snap your bones
for all you know
your paper airplanes
have kinder trajectories
man, I've never had your arm

Did You Move the Coffee Pot

in your dream
and can you fall asleep
so we can have it back

did you float back up
from underwater
to the skin of your quilt

did you finish our argument
in your sleep
did you replace the milk, then

was there roadkill there
is it animated here
did you name the pets in *Nod*

do they come
when you call
in the cognizant now

is the language
still the same
on their tags

were there planes overhead
did it feel like a room
did the jets echo in there

which way did the toilets flush
did the food taste like itself
was it new

was the play
inside itself
a better reflection of you

did the spoons ripple
did the songs oscillate
and when you put your glasses down

could you still read
or hear someone on the other end
of the fancy telephone

when they called
are we them
are you able to speak

My Soul is Unfortunately a Bird

my childhood was a bar of gold
it's a cliché, but my brother and I fight
like cats and dogs
and when it storms hammers
and nails
out back
in piles

we look out
from in between the drapes
and say *it looks like rain*
it sounds like a bowling alley
and when the cats and dogs
return to us in sheets
we name them

I am
undeniably
an Audubon
every bird my soul has ever been
contains its own multitudes
to hide the shame, every sparrow
has stood inside a novel
bird's shadow

when I search the reference books
for synonyms for
what my soul has always been
it always comes up
bird, bird, bird
I will never escape that designation
librarians have always shooed me outdoors
towards where they keep
guidebooks for birders
in the bookcases within the branches
of the library trees

but contrary to the feral things
I've always been
constrained by alphabets
and don't think I haven't asked
to be let in on their secret grammars
I'm always jealous of cicadas
whose cat calls
last for years, in ricochets
there are beasts whose childhoods
have never been
battened down by metaphors
there are birds
whose souls are hollow
or so I've heard
I think, *those lucky*
little devils

Old Make of the Old Car

I know who you are
I haven't crossed you
by accident

wind chimes, chiming
in the Octobered dawn
your voice, as familiar as boyhood

box of wine behind
less conspicuous cardboard
your face is how I remember it

father, brother, Mom
try as I might, to remove you
you Oldsmobile out

you clang with the dwindling birdsong
your stains remain
your blushes corrugate

weathered belt
don't pretend I don't know you
fish hook, don't birthday with me

cry on the midnight playground
don't messaround
I know the moment I cried you

dumb Irish jig in the kitchen
you are as bad
as you are

claws in the cushions
there's no use
in choring you out

I know the threads in a blindfold
I knew the kid
hidden there

shelter creaks
there's no money
piled high

enough to forget you
you are still there
brother, nephew, child

that sound as yours
as mine, is there
no shade enough

to clear out its shadow, old car
you only go home, to
fall to pieces in breadcrumbs

don't guardrail with me
don't spade around
we both know who shot the moon

it wasn't you
daughter, grandkid, Pop
you know

which way the trouble will roll
this year, or a thousand nexts
don't genuflect with me

there's no need to doctorate around it
we see those teeth
in the candles and cake

don't mistake kindness for hunger
pang-for-pang
I know the zig of your scars

they're ours
don't snowflake with us
don't lawyer up

we know your bible from ours
by the tears in the pages
there's no way

to apocrypha out
of the same old jelly and jam
those seeds don't hunt

those sticks don't nun
you get me
old car this far

north of the plot
James, Madeline, me
play the hits

like you did
when you were just kids
don't you orphanage

there's enough of us
to go around
you'll never count

every leaf in that tree
every jumper, every *say Uncle, jack*
you'll never get back to one

one thousand, two
you only get
one blitz

and you used yours
somewhere outside of Buffalo
or should I say *wasted*

you can't entendre an entendree
you get me
you don't get to title

the one about the car
that zombied around
every town I've ever hid

sister, Son
who never lived
don't bury the chart

split open the organ
and fiddle
with its nuts and bolts

that's not where the song is
where it hums
don't tinker or bee

if you hit that old relic
with the side of a wrench
its nose won't glow

it's a stone
a story best left unresurrected
as out of place

as your old man's belt
a *she* set of keys
a shudder that escapes

when they say they have
each other's eyes
wrapped around

two fingers
a breast
a pocket, a waist

Hitchhiking to Canaan

back at home, my brother is in splinters
his mother is a gin-soaked bathrobe
draped over a tub
or a stump of an old tree
where a historic storm
once gave a homily

I can hear the termites
hacking away
at the studs behind
our laundry room
even though I'm miles away
and at liberty
to hear nothing

I was born with eyes too wide
sworn to an Irish secrecy
which only means that I've been an inquisition
a question made of family portraits
I was a middler
made from risk and intent
I was a speck on the hand
I wore the soil in its uniform

back at home, my father is a set of bald tires
a tongue of fire burns above the mailbox
a patch of dirt depicts the property line
where nobody dares to leave a glove out in the rain
I am a passenger on an interstate
and I make note to never inquire
the driver of his name
I try to imagine a baptism
during these violent plunges
into what might be Virginia

in the future I might thank myself
for the risk
but I am a kid
who cannot see his hand beyond his face
and so I regret almost everyone
and in me is born a great empathy
when I give my name to motorists
it doesn't sound like prayer

I make mention
of every village
as its first brick is placed beside its sibling
and when I pray I ask the towns
be stricken from their interstates
and tunnels from the mountains
and when I'm brave
I hold my breath
as explosions carve an artery
through my belly
and inside the passing homes
receivers are stripped
from their blurry telephones

In the Photo of You

wearing your little league grin
propped up against a sibling
laughing at a harmless slight
long forgotten
in the trunk
of a starter car
with northern plates
playing a classic song
through the transistors

    you're forgiven

just out of the local parish
during the casserole part of the day
with a glint of swimming lessons
in your eye
and plenty of trust
reflected in your brother's
say cheese expression

    you're part of God's plan

the glitches in your heart
are what makes you extraordinary
in the hospital of your parents' terrors
down the hall from makeshift uncles
you're still a key ingredient
in the Jesus soup

    but today, you aren't

you're our mother's first broken egg
and betrayal is your vocation
I'm sure they hung a name
over your crib
and once, I knew its meaning
but if I were a betting man

I'd venture to say you didn't live up to it
that worms have hollowed out
its rounder consonants

I like to look at pictures of you, smiling
in those photos
we're just Pharaoh and Moses
as kids
we haven't yet pulled magic into our sticks
they're just for practice
and couldn't cleave a puddle
for more than a few seconds

in that still universe
framed in my hallway
you've still got all of your authentic parts
and I don't count the cities I've placed between us

     as blessings

I Never Thought of Myself as Much of a Gardener

      1.

yesterday, I flipped through the want ads
like a child
who spins a globe and lands on his hometown

and—true to form—I found myself peering out through the newsprint
and grinned
in response to the wording of my post

I wondered the timeline of my inquiry
and sighed in laughter
when I asked myself to come *kick the tires*
give the old traveler
another crack at the wheel

      2.

you never give the body much thought
until you find yourself staring out dumbly
through a few feet of stagnant summer air
and wondering about the scattered limbs of your own meandering arteries
or the trunk width
of your trachea

you don't pray anymore
but you sometimes find yourself
in conversation with
the sum of hearing you've misplaced
or the fuzzy glow
of deer eyes in
in the low tide
of your night vision
or even a bottleneck of kids
lining up at an icee cart
when the attendant's bell sounds
and you don't salivate

3.

I'd be lying if I told you that curiosity
hadn't gotten the best of me

(it has)

you'd be surprised if you found yourself
at your own interview
looking back across a soft wooden plain

I am not a good liar
but I can be convincing
in times of an emergency

turns out
if I need an extension
I can apply for one
should the river rise
my chair will double
as a flotation device

4.

you don't give curiosity its due
when your kid asks you
about the separate, but equally disturbing
totalities of gravities it takes
to keep the sun fed
and a black hole, cottonmouthed

but it does make you think about the *skin* of water
had it more of a consciousness
you imagine
water wouldn't have named it *skin,* at all
if you put a plain between a half-filled glass
and everything surrounding it
and turn it upside down
and take away the overlay

it holds itself in
it's an old parlor trick

the ocean has the atmosphere, you think
it takes a lot of pride
to defy letting go

      5.

I never thought of myself as much of a gardener
but this summer I grew some tomatoes

and I found myself flipping through the possibilities
as I stewed
the harvested *heirlooms*
and married them to an old recipe

as I let the ingredients do their best
to live up to the hype
an old friend reached out to me
to ask about an old stanza
I'd once assembled
and did *my* best
to bring a few folks back to life
but all I could do
was make a real-time observation
about the state of tomatoes

lovingly, I mentioned that the skin of a black hole
can be two dimensional
and information can be stored there
like a recipe or a photograph
for every infinite gardener
an infinite harvest

6.

you remember that game
we all played where you'd spin a globe
try your hardest to cheat
and put a heavy finger on home

memories are funny
now that globes are extinct
the slower you spun the Earth
the easier it was to fix the game

I've read that they used to warp the continents
depending on where the globemakers were from
so you could get it right
but, unbeknownst to anyone
the outcome would still be rigged

you ever thought about putting a globe
on a platter
closing your eyes
and giving it a good shake
only to open them back up
for a snapshot of a moment

you ever tried to summarize
the sum of a full day's ecstasy and grief
you'd have to be a good gardener
to put your hand into that hat
and acquire any semblance of the truth

it's like that game we used to play
where you'd take yourself out for a spin
and pass your house a thousand times
and each time the people inside
betrayed each other a little less
and despite their best attempts
they became strangers

if you could see the big picture
you wouldn't hold those efforts
against them

they don't put faults on globes
for good reason

you ever wonder if there's a museum
dedicated to the anthropology of globes
or how heavy a roomful of lead balloons
would look
if you were made subject to it

you ever wonder about the orbit of your character
or the hot mess of a story
that's told from the cradle to a pirouette

    7.

I haven't

I've only just learned the name of the *cabbage moths*
that visit us overnight
like terrible thieves
putting a little daylight
between our thumbs and efforts
for all I know
it's the same hungry soul
every time

I never imagined myself
that curious
a traveler
to ever trace a line of tomatoes
from out back to the Spanish
then the Aztecs, or even earlier

before Eden was a myth
and back when they were still poisonous

On a Mattress We Couldn't Replace

in the house we tried to buy
with the stove that burned
borrowed gas

ten feet from an unturned garden
one hundred miles north
of a slow government heist

a week before any paycheck
a day after another pipe froze
on the taxman's birthday

while the water fell
into saucepans without sauce
into distended tupperware bowls

as the moths danced safely
in deposit boxes
as two cats tugged on a sweater thread

that ran along a broken tile
up a cord once filled with conversation
you said

at least we have our health
and it sounded like a Christmas Eve
from sometime in our childhoods

when the men had come to fix our mother
and the old man put below the tree
a worn out oxhide baseball glove

Dear Wife,

it's dusk
and the sky is yellow
and the sky is green, also
we cannot decide

our daughter is coloring the stoop stairs
with chalk
because it's April
and the weather cannot
figure itself out, either
you pull on a sweater
that was once mine
but has since shrunk
to almost your size

we are listening for the familiar sounds
of the ice cream truck
our daughter has quarters
stacked like drunk towers
on the stairs' railing

we've brought a small speaker
out from the den
and Simon and Garfunkel
are in Central Park
singing a song about home

our daughter gives up
and runs up the street to the bodega
we let her imagine she's free
to do this on her own
but trailing her
in a pair of socks
I pretend that I am
a gumshoe

the clerk gives her small frame a boost
so she can reach down
into the bottom of the freezer
and once she has paid
he comes to the propped door
and raises his hand to signify
that he has distinguished her father
and softly waves at me
from across the street
our daughter pantomimes
looking both ways
because, for her
this is an important
first of many firsts

I ask her if she has counted her change
which she ignores and instead
lets me in on the fact that
her popsicle is multi-layered
which signifies that she has made
a wise purchase
not only does her *firework*
cover all the regular bases
but it also entertains the senses
below the surface

we get back to the stoop
to continue to shoot the April breeze
and I place your feet back in my lap
the ice cream truck
eventually passes
and I swear
that if God, himself
were to descend before us
to take me home
I would fight him
right there, in the street

I Would Like to Have Entered the Kitchen

but by the time I had reached
the shadows of its fan blades

it had become only the lore
of thrown spaghetti

so I made my way through
the old laughter

to our office
expecting both of our desks

to be sitting snugly where
we had left them

like two cross bananas
but only a waterbug could be found

curiously typing out utility bills
for the family we once were

as I stepped among the remaining tiles
the umbrellas all shared their long standing

opinions on the state of the vestibule
and when I finally reached my old chair

below the photographs
I sat and wondered their expressions

without the courage to look up and into
their illegible grins

knowing every hospital visit
every loose tooth

might not be there
to greet my gaze

Now is Always Escaping Me

yesterday I planted matchbox cars in the garden
come tomorrow
we can escape the waters
lapping at the vault doors
they installed on the battery

a few weeks ago I packed a parachute
in place of my kid's textbooks
it's funny how the word *vital*
can be taken
for *granted*
last night I dreamt that we were falling
and when we pulled the ripcord
books spilled out around us
their pages, reaching skyward
like arms in prayer

this morning I woke
from a dream about the nonsense
we pack away in vaults
in the foothills of our memories
I knocked the sand off my pajamas
and went out to see
if even a fender had sprouted
between the flowers
that shone like an oil slick
amidst the weeds that grew
as if no one was left
to discriminate
the goats from the sheep

Watching the Cryptographers

cricket, she said
mean*s I love you*

and *pineapple* means
we've met once before
but we were siblings, then
we will all be siblings

dungarees is *everything has already happened*
but also means *bar fight*
and sometimes just *saloon*
and even *the swinging of a door*

cypher means *to hear*
so when I say *decipher*
it means *stop listening*
but always understand
and *understand* combined with *I*
means *start over*

sibling means *connected by tragedies*
but if you want to be less hyperbolic
it can also mean *sign language*
and *translator*
and oftentimes *ceremony*
so to have a sibling
means *to have a quiet ceremony*

do you understand, she asked

cricket, I said. cricket

I Name This Scar My Brother

I call the house we tried to topple
Jericho

the cotton between the arguments
I call *The Holy Ghost*

we *modified our Saharas*
by the grass stains in our jeans

every crawdad
was a kraken

every home we turned our backs on
eventually became salt

my old man used to wear a serpent
to hold his pants in place

every birthday was a Pentecost
every pencil held a pentagram

every deep-end seemed to magnify
the angles of our animals

when God was just a dog ear
in the epilogue

a curfew that escapes
when the window breaks

a forgotten knot on a bed sheet
like scattered beads

between the car seats
from a broken dashboard rosary

we were told sainthood
required three miracles

so we rode our bikes
with our arms crossed like pharaohs

across our concave chests
we puffed them out like roosters

as we passed our annual
roman candle tests

we changed out of our uniforms
into alter robes

in the gauntlets of the rectories
squeaking past the minotaurs

where, in the land of children
the one-eyed priest was king

I name this wound, my brother
the one he couldn't shield

from the stubbled hour he spent
dozing beneath the fabled tree

to the year he began to shave
in the era of hollowed-out bibles

when magazines hid
in magazines

every sibling has a gap in his childhood
every sapling

an emergent tooth
on the timberline

there are miracles you have to perform
without gods

days you have to escape
by ignorance

sometimes a rite of passage
aligns with another's viaticum

sometimes what you thought was water
isn't water

when your brother
hands you a flask

and says, *here*
drink this

I Began to Wonder

if I, myself
was one of the three Joannas

or if after three long Joannas
we'd roll away the stone

and there would be none
and which of those two scenarios was worse

in the process, I tried on the second Joanna
to see if anyone would even notice

sure, it was creepy
but put yourself in my shoes

ask yourself what you'd do
if Joanna was an actual option

but mid-Joanna
and after very little research

I realized I was wanted in Wisconsin
so I ditched the aforementioned

Joanna, and went with the third
I acquired the patience for soccer

for once in my life
I enjoyed a stiff martini

and please don't judge
lest you be Joanna

The First
and before you even ask

yes,
being recognized as the original recipe

is as terrifying
as it sounds

I'm Old Enough

to know
seeds lie
in wait
and some
like me
have been
simmering
in their beds
not far
from where
they were
surrendered to
a future stock
where some
Johnny Appleseed
said here
as a distant gaze
spread across his
apple face
I hope
your stalks
stretch further
than this
and in my
mind, they do
my thoughts
find yours
mid-reach
and agree
like sycophants
tend to
and somewhere
along our accord
when our egos
have long since
softened
you

say *farther*
and I say
*I know
how
was I
supposed
to drum
up a cue
but to
offer
some low
hanging fruit*

On Second Thought

it's possible that I was neither
the second Joanna, nor the third
and the first was owed an explanation

for disparaging her
already reckless soul
while borrowing the keys

because I knew the deal
I was still
myself

as knowing mechanism
as auxiliary, horrified Joannas
watched along

but you never know
we could be talking smoke
there's always a chance

that the mirrors bent
in such a way
that access to me became attainable

maybe my rusty kickstand
had begged the ether, replete
and corresponding disturbances

were tumbling in the silt
by virtue of the light coming through a window
where any guess would lead

to: Joanna as inspiration
of *on second thought, Joanna*
I apologize

for wherever I discarded you
along your trajectory
the last thought I can attest to

wasn't guilt or anxiety
but a keen sense of obligation
to the burners

on the range in a home
I'd clean forgot
along my Joanna way

The Devil and Robert Johnson

*"The very study of the external world led to the conclusion
that the content of the consciousness is an ultimate reality."*

because I am cinders of you
who passed through my door

died on my watch
leapt into my swimming arms

I am obliged to proclaim our fleeting union
my debt is unfathomable

being prom dress and open heart surgery
the new can smell of tennis balls

dead birds and
copperheads buried in a pile of maple leaves

and the night it took you to pick
a fish out of the bog

the hours it took to descale it
kill it against a tree

and devour it whole
I am the *after* of that

I am a leathery swig of scotch
halfway through a recent funeral

my father's shoddy belt
his mother's bible pencil

and somehow, a frozen gerbil
behind an old tottering shed

nothing has been this stew
quite like I have

nobody declared amnesty
behind the sacred doors of Honda Accords

quite like
I did that summer I tried to wear

someone else's diary
and came back a stranger, anyhow

they can't reassemble the cistern
of holy water

from that moment my folks
promised me to God

or the reluctance
I've fashioned in my mind

to travel anywhere of blessed merit
they haven't pushed my stone

In the Dream Where You Were Me

you lumbered through
my commute

in bones like mine
without my acclimations

rain hit my face
in our mind, early

you argued with your myself
over trains, directions

felt at your collar
where a rosary doesn't hang

you took my coffee
with that look of yours on my face

on the phone you thought
my old man sounded miserable

half-strangers near our daughter's school
scowled

when absently
you didn't return pleasantries

you played with our wedding band
you carried our child on my shoulders

you loved her in my separate way
you strong-armed the stand clear doors

thought longingly about me
where back at home

I quietly wept
drinking your tea

There is a Thin Knot

that hangs
in a room

where I have stopped sending my mail
and while I imagine

a jam has built up
in the queue

in its place
or possibly somewhere alongside it

I've scared up a supernova
upon which I've scribbled

a grocery list;
a long and winding diversion

I've lost track of how long
my thoughts have thinned there

to become vivid or kelp
or terrible swimmers

the knot is a grayed talisman
but in my flight of fancy

it has silvered
like a baby's spoon

is not used on a baby
and instead sits in the silverware drawer

like Joseph in a well
like a title does on a book

bored to death
by misuse

Much Like Edith

we turned around
to take one last look at the mountain

thunder in our legs
fireflies skimming the high grasses

our mouths, worn down
by their own metrical sounds

I wondered how much of your childhood
was gone for good

hungry
you sat in the mountain's valley

an emergent woman
emanating from your gaze

we tried to predict the sequence
of the strobing insects

by their trajectories
as the bats

began to chirp
against an invisible lid

the shadows rang
and the mountain was annexed

by the dimming tree line
but we lingered

as if the city had no more use for us
and the mountain

had already loaned us
its tallest buildings

Every Time I Pass the Room in Manhattan Where My Daughter Was Born

it gets me to we wondering
if a violinist
while stringing her instrument

can hear a mourning note
when she's going through
the motions

it reminds me of the fact
that in any city of merit
there's usually a river

you can attach
to more than one generation
a place where children have swum

with their fathers' ghosts
I get this feeling
when my old man is laughing

that there's other tremors
just below the surface
a hiccup in the heartbeat

where the longer parts of stories
are told
I have this chair in the parlor

where a crocheted blanket
lounges like a ghost
where my body goes

after a clock has been beaten
to a pulp
it's the place where my daughter

sometimes falls asleep
after clicking her tongue along
with my irregular pulse

I get this intuition
that I should feel lucky
during the routines of any night

that cutting carrots
seven inches from my wife
while she makes a broth

and hums along to the radio
are the closest moments
I have to prayers

I get this feeling that our reel
is simmering
above the surface of its double, where

sometimes I'm the body;
sometimes I'm the thing
caught inside

All of the Sudden

gray hairs have sprouted in the bath
the mirrors have their say

kids tend to need
more than you can give

pillow fights leave a scar
long pauses in correspondence

lead to longer pauses
the old dish breaks in the sink

the fork and the spoon blush
when you say

could be an omen
another wedding present

is hurried away with a dustpan
another carpet has sprung a lump

and a line of ants
leading a path to the hill

carries another poem back to their den
one letter after the next

I Haven't Laughed Like That in Years

I watched your hands toy
with the drag
out of the passenger side window
noted the mile marker
where a hotel sign
grew like a weed
high above the pines
as you craned your head back
to keep it in view

held your finger so
as you dozed
and when you tumbled out of your dream
to bouts of laughter
I was embittered
a pinch

I haven't similarly
cornered myself in *Nod*
for longer than I'd dare admit
some of my old fits
have been swallowed
whole by the elbows
so tonight, on our long journey home
when you lost your shit
I held my sandpaper grin in my hands
consumed in earnest, by equal parts
adoration and jealousy

In the Dream You Said

he's picking out which memories
to keep

like they were blurry negatives
wet and hung on a line

you were in the kitchen
dancing with the saucepans

while the calicoes
bent their ears

the sound of bare toes clung
to the tiles

I was dreaming of being anything
picking out which light bulbs

to be blown
pulling up the table leaves

vacuuming up the horseshoes
when luck came unattached; I was

gathering an alphabet
from the harp strings of our song

making wisecracks
about the cinders

from a broadcast
of the trance

What We Weren't Told About the Middle

the hospitals would know us
by our first names

days would become
monthsyearsdecades

we would see toddlers
in our teenagers' eyes

people would inevitably die
eventually, we'd survive

our hopes would realistically drown
but would return to us in Sunday clothes

religions would lose their long standing wars
with time

half of our married friends
would raise their children on the weekends

our dreams would be realized
too soon

but they'd accompany
castles we'd built by grudges

and various shapes and sizes
of since-lowered caskets

we would know the middle
by our presence within it

we would become *middlers*
when we realized

the lies we were paid
when our elders said

they'd *picked no favorites*
were gracious

and we'd empathize
when running our fingers

through our favored child's hair
that's how the middle is known

it's bearing the weight of a Christmas fable
until it can no longer hold

and asking the eldest
not to spoil it for his sister

it's not answering the phone
when the news is a bombshell

in the middle
of the night

when it isn't drunk friends
but sober ones

it's numbers on a cake
instead of individual candles

the elders spared us
when they forgot

the deaths that came as surprises
the cancers and the gunshots

that ricocheted off the cement blocks
in First Grade classrooms

but when we become *middlers*
it sinks in

you get the voicemail
and it's your best mate's wife

and she says, her voice shaking
hey, it's me

you gotta come
I'm not sure if he's gonna make it

and you buy the next flight
right to the heart, the center of it

although you weren't told
how sharp the middle could be

but who could blame anyone
for keeping it in

would you travel here, now
knowing what you know

What I Have Put in Place of *Church*

I have become a wholesaler of terms

the time before I turn on the car
before I carry out myself for a day
has replaced *litany*

the moment when a creature
doesn't bolt into the refuge
has taken the place of *faith*

when I attend a wedding or funeral
and employ the craftwork of poetry for the feast
I've taken *tourist* and *thief*
from the gaze of the parishioners
and put *Samaritan* and *plagiarist*
in their stead

so far I've worked out
that the word *Confirmation*
has become *citizen*

in proxy to this practice
seedling
has been traded for *reconciliation*
and *gestation* has taken its place in the Bible
where the *Stations of the Cross* have been sourced

and I'm still trying to find
something more kinetic
more strapped to inertia
to replace the concept of *exile*
something far less subversive than *exorcist*
but packs more of a punch than *bridge*

Try to Imagine Me

sitting here in the driver's seat
windshield wipers blazing
fumbling with the bear's head
hissing
cuss words through my teeth
no zippers
no arrow,
instructing which end goes where
no holes in the sockets

are you here
can you feel my heart rate
does the steering wheel
feel like a battering ram
the bucket seat, a straight jacket
are you asking yourself how
we've arrived at this destination
never mind the head

there are school pictures taped to the dash
somebody has purchased an air freshener
there's some sort of device
that pays the bridge tolls
Jumping Jesus
there is a whole circuitry
cobbled together with hot glue
it's not the fish flopping in my lap
or the river pumped into
the navigation system's pinhole speaker

it's the sensible man
that our audience finds unbelievable
when they discover that he's been baptized
when he extracts a spring-loaded trap
from the glovebox
and all of its functions dawn
its teeth bared in a wisecrack

its catch wagging like a tongue
will you remain
can you just sit here for awhile
while we practice our grunts

Schrödinger's Karl

it was in that world that I dared myself
to admit that a body that contained me
was there

that the poem that contained that dare
had letters that could briefly trail a premonition

and of course, there was us
and we agreed to get dressed
and we agreed on the rules
and we set our clocks to each other

separately, we dared to have a father
to believe in the gospel of lineage
to adopt his defects
to suffer his lust

it was in that era that we carved out neighbors
and wore party hats and sang *happy birthday*

we marked the properties with a line
and then drew up a mountain range
or a river
to keep our boundaries in check
we planted ourselves behind windows
and whatever grew, fermented
we put a cat in the tomb
to keep our loose souls company
and placed all the other creatures
in our fare

we harnessed clouds
and colored animals inside the lines
while the Earth fed our nocturnal urges
so it could tell a story of us
to those who persisted

I was a thing that wrote itself
and because I could mourn him
I could mourn the old invisible bricks
and all the faith that eked
from mustard seeds
unspool any creed
by traveling backwards
become my own mother
name myself
become a mote
between one digit
and the infinite

My Father is Over There

in an upholstered wooden chair
looking at photographs of the day
over his reading glasses
asking the simulated person in his phone
the longitude and latitude of Dublin

I am on a sofa bed
reading, below a painting of a pale and naked body
with ribbon red nipples
loosely peripherizing the whole scene

this morning, to no one in particular
he said
at the arrivals gate
I am in Ireland
like he was casting a spell
or phoning a younger version of himself

I have not yet learned how to masterfully weave
my story between the heavy threads of an older one
but he is teaching me

when we walk along the river
in search of some nucleus
I watch him run his fingers
across the goose flesh cement
of the barrier fence
like he is reading the city's fortune

we will not travel here again
even though the rain holds up
and our backs are treated to an old blessing
we will not break the spell
by playing any low keys

I leave a book I am reading
on our host's bookcase
write her a short note to
thank her
and every other mouth, body
and set of eyes
that I've encountered
here in this arcane nation

where I am afraid to wake up
where I am only awake, on this sofa
listening to the sounds of my father
as he rubs his sore calves
and compares the climates of here and home

The Weak Binary

it's not all black and white
it's not black and white at all
it's not ever black and white

the flashpoints don't always make it
past the editors
so-to-speak

I have this worst memory
I take out from time to time
to examine

and wonder who I'd be if I'd buried it
if I'd slept through the details
or the perpetrators were bit parts

the point is, I cannot best it
or strip it of its confusion
or put it in a dress

it neither defines me
or cuts me loose
but there was a single moment

when I realized that childhood was a farce
it was then I became a thief
stealing joy wherever I could fathom it

I became careful
not to strip it from anyone
who needed it

I was the kid behind the couch
every Christmas
hoping beyond hope that the fictions were true

I know the cost of a bicycle
is a marriage
an oil change, a suicidal hour at the store

there are days when my mother
is wearing more
and there are moments when I'm brave

enough to lead her naked body
from the confines
of a tennis court

I Wish

I had some metal in my head
I could rap my fist on and say *oh that
that's nothing*

you should see the place
where my mind used to set up
shop, roots, or lay down
a primer coat
it's just this metal plate
sitting on a bias like a valentine

it gets tricky, sometimes
on my side of the moon
when I try
to carve out
the punchlines

don't mind me

I've got this nifty parlor trick
where I take it out
and use it as a shaving mirror
or to make sure my trident
is cocked just right

I Am Not the Man

I was this morning
I don't recognize
the person who woke
made eggs
drank the leftover coffee
from the fridge

I am not the son you raised
the voter you paid
the husband you married
the father you wanted

I am most certainly
not the brother who loved you
you are not the hero
I had hoped you'd become
I don't have a pocket full of dog treats
today

even if I did
I would give them freely
to some other dog
who begged on his knees
of some other me

I Would Like to Believe

that if I nodded off
on your shoulder

mid-poem
that you would return the favor

and pick it up
off my lap

and continue reading
where I left off

and while we are here
in the fork of this memory

I'd also like to submit
that the poem in the dream

continued on your shoulder
would be far better

than the original
you'd be obliged to sustain

the remix
would contain a list of birds

my daughter would often recite
on our way down to the station

the *Red-Tailed Hawk*
of my fancy

would be far more
red-tailed

than our local fellow
and because the dreamed bits

often go off the rails
with me

by the end
when I woke

and you cracked a grin
the raptor made only

of fan belts and shoestrings
would be

in hot pursuit
of me

II. Concerning Midnight Gardeners

yesterday I saw a man/who looked like/he could belong to/a distant century/except for his face mask/and plastic bag/stop and pull peonies/out of that bag/and lay them on the bumper/of a refrigerated corpse truck/humming behind a funeral home/and look up at the sky/above the corpse truck/with dignity and ceremony
—Denver Butson

She Waters the Cilantro

during these not-normal times
we take walks up to the bodega

noting
the new mail carrier

wondering
what might've happened to the last

we order in
food we cannot afford

tip more than we dare
take longer than we should in the store

run our hands over the ridges on the cans
our tongues over the grooves

of the bottles' mouths
in times, abnormal

we stop at a stoop
we've passed a hundred times before

share stories we've never ran the risk
of hearing aloud, until now

we pause, work out smiles with our eyes
frowns with our hands

in uneven nights
on sleepless dawns

we call and call and call
hundred-year friends

who pick up
most of the time

on avant-hours
when candy is sharper

savoring
ice cream, colder than you've ever had

under airplane-less skies
before boatless harbors

we love
all the way down

from our ruddy throats
to the tips of our lashes

we make it to
the evenings we are in

tending
midnight gardens

while watering the bulbs
our weary minds grow

threadbare and aware
that it shows

Being a Taxi Driver is Hard Work

first you have to be born a taxi driver
and forget the language you spoke

when you were a midwife
in one century, or another

then, you have to teach yourself
to drive a bull between upright clowns

and pan for gold medallions
on the Hudson River shore

and watch your fortune
rise and fall

with the advent of the headless coachmen
and the pixelated passengers

drawn by artists
in the satellites

and there's always strawberry milkshake residue
caked between the vinyl faults

and every other weekend
you have to chop down a four inch pine

and hang it from
the rearview mirror

so the passengers can fill their heads
with evergreen nostalgia

and you have to suffer the nuptials
the honeymoon and the divorce

that happens every Saturday
between Saint Marks Avenue and 84th

you have to travel back in time
and rename the glove box

something more appropriate
like *things you only show the cops* box

you have to remember to forget
which direction Mecca is

while you're listening to a passenger
recall the Wailing Wall

reminding you, incessantly
which way up, Downtown is

and you have to start a fire
each night in Queens

with lotto stubs and greyhound dreams
to warm the moons across your knuckles

the sun painted across your
taxi driver hands

at ten and two, during
the prime meridian of your shift

What We'll Do

we'll go down to that storied river
in your famous town
if you walk far enough
there should be one of both

and we'll see the kids we've abandoned
in the water looking up
and we will cotton candy
and we will cherry bomb the swings
and we will shirts
and we will skins

we will taste our old man's catcher's mitt
play a cassette in our brother's stolen player
we will take off as many layers
as we dare
and we will curse the clinics
for stealing every other minute
and we will name the kids
who scared us into them

and we will practice drowning
and we will butterfly the heights
knifing at our guts
and fall asleep in cars
drink anything
we can get our hands on
and find the courage
to rent a place in other states
and return when someone's dying
and find the words to bury them

we will become people
we'll apologize for
and settle in
to fearful ways
we'll be shitty on the phone

hear our recorded voices
tremble at our mother's timbre
try our keys in every lock
drunk down to the bone

the famous town will lose its luster
forget the hairpins in its lore
and you'll be nicked
when someone says the river
looks like any other
while the cemeteries blend
while the clinics get religion
while the sidewalks pile with evergreens
and down the streets, tinsel tumbleweeds

and we will what we did
drum the old nicknames into our kids
we will straighten out
the dog ears in the Gospels
and we will test the bottles
on our naked upturned wrists
name people names we wished

but
we once cotton candied
we once Wonder Wheeled
we once walked ourselves
into desperate cities
and clawed out lives
from our imaginations

and had to ask the natives
the name that was the river
we'd soon look over
begging it
to reflect our first set
of baby teeth

The Cat is Old

there's only one drop of milk
in the carton
the school is on the phone
about a *fat lip*
and an *ice pack*
but you're underground
it could be an ice pick
it could be lice

an old friend
has died
and the doctor is angry
that you've asked him
for a cure
there are no pills
for suffering

your friend says with a laugh
in the future
they will call these moments memories

the cat is old
you say
to a child
who is yours
instead of saying
Zoie died
and we are never getting over it
we'll just get old, too
become accustomed
to the passages

the patio
has committed suicide
the vines have twisted
like worms into the shed

the oven
has sabotaged the leftovers
and the place down the street
is saying there will be
a thirty minute wait
for another version
of the meal you've murdered
back home
where the wait
is accompanied by
an old wanton cat

the cereal
looks like life preservers
the light is out in the bathroom
the clerk at the hardware store
has passed out in the drawer marked
miscellaneously sized screws
the police are in the street
surrounding a man in a Riker's uniform
with a pile of your unpaid bills
at his feet
they ask if you recognize him
reluctantly, you say
you recognize the electric bill
noticing the envelope
is lighter than the last
by one bathroom's amount of luminosity

the cat is old
but to her, it's nothing
she steps into the rain
like it's raining for the first time
and so it is
when she looks up
with her best
what the fuck face
and I shoot back a
don't ask me, sister look

I was just put
in this day
in this allotment
of joy and suffering

I say to the room
someone toss me some cereal
I think my daughter
has a case of the ice picks
but I'm hard of hearing
and wondering where Zoie's gone
if she's nudging adjectives
off a cloud
and muttering the words
lightning in a bottle
like it's the first time
we've ever heard them

the cat is the cat
and every time the sun
warms a square foot of flooring
in the parlor
it's the first time

even though
people have died before
I mean to say, *instead*
the sun has crossed overhead
for the last time
for some

They Made Us Humans

when it would've been easier to be aardvarks
not to vote or write songs

or fall on any hand grenades
or spend so many hours

wishing
we were geese

studying
their playbooks

naming
a creation

that never wished at all
or practiced plastic surgery

they put bricks
around a door

and gave us
a set of keys

so, we bought an expensive chair
and sat in it

until we could work out
a first draft

early sketches of a piano
a prison to put birdsong in

we sat there writing poetry
until one of us wondered

who was the first
to die in Nagasaki

who caught the bomb
on the head

was he
wishing

to be
an aardvark, all along

was he midway
through a song

When I Write the Older Gentleman Into the Poem

I call him
the older gentlemen

who fumbles with his keys
like they are coins for an offering plate

when he says they won't work
they are his faithful keys

in the poem
I work out their betrayal

and when the sweat beads on his glasses
the sweat beads on his glasses

he is as frozen as he is frozen
in the poem he becomes

king of the vestibule
when I tell him that one day

the buzzards will come
in the poem, it's a buzzer

connected as freely to a tenant's finger
as a light switch might be

to a chair
in a prison

when I stand at the elevator door
I do so

like a loosened
bobcat might

if it had a view of a city, perhaps
but the elevator inside the mountain

isn't for me

Sunset Park

and *God's Away*
On Business

was playing
through broken speakers

while the paleteros were making like
it was the Daytona 500

while unidentified children sold
UFOs

to other children
before the fireworks show

and halfway down the hill
somebody inflated a movie theatre

when the dialogue thundered
down past the bricks and dipped

its toes
in the river

I swear we saw bodega cats
walking on churros like they were stilts

there was a balloon war
when the handball court broke

into a round of applause
as shower shoes were tossed

into the sky
like they were mortarboards

somebody played a plastic trumpet
while some kid on grips

cut the power to
an artificial sun

when the pedestrians blinked
we walked straight through

a knife fight like
we were Israelites

and, swear to God
the crackling under our shoes

happened to be actual
paper money

from every corner
of the world

On Not Seeing the Red Bird Off the Coast of Argentina

having never picked glass off a church pew
I venture bravely into places which

aren't Argentina
though I have seen a red bird

and have come close to Buenos Aires, once
by way of forcing a wooden raft

down the Uruguay River of my dreams
although I didn't recognize

its *Uruguayness* until I traced a finger
down the hypotheses of its rapids

most things that have yet to be done
I haven't and will likely never

so the unicycle tells it
for which the dodo cries

all the red birds!
not one Argentine

and thus runners-up
in my own private drag show

with regards to red birds off of Argentina's coast
I have missed the boat

and while I could ease my shame
by naming

each and every gecko
that once looked through

our mosquito curtains
I will refrain

from dabbing at the stains
on the impossibly unswept glass

with the curious rag
tucked near the lapel

on
my fabricated coat

Vestiges

in concert with the 17 year cicadas
climbing out of their tombs

local mermaids
are ungluing their scales

pinning them back
to the prom dresses from whence they came

somebody drops a pair of maracas
over heaven's ledge

and I find it hard to believe
it's accidental

that the parade calls out sick
at the very moment

the dead decide
to spruce up their wings with talcum powder

when the paper peals
off a few magnetic boulders

intended for
seaworn sailors

as the tree limbs glimmer
like pennies in the sun

for every mermaid
an equal and opposite cicada to take her place

each faster than the last
to steal the rattle off a rattlesnake

this would be the year
to swallow shadows whole

and catch glockenspiels
between our toes

like it was our one and only
parlor trick

More Than Ever

I need to see that red bird
off the coast of Argentina

whose songs pick clefs from the lye
what games were we playing

that our boats didn't take us there
where the painted stones

are scaled in Bible verse
too groggy in the ear

to do us any harm
red bird, the reddest bird on record

cancer red
red as a lion's tongue

what address did you write
on our forfeit invitation

one hundred million angels
in your prow

bellyful of plague
what morons we were

to hide our shame in crossword puzzles
for not having flattened your map

rabbit's eye red
red as a blood bank

like Mother Theresa
your watchers, myriad

lounging in the periphery
like tourists

fiddling with their coffee spoons
reddest bird of Argentine descent

I can hear
stray dogs snapping at horse flies

sirens in the sea caves
red birds in the sun

backlit like cars
in a funeral cortege

siblings
against the canopy

your audience, a bandshell
of sailor's warning clouds

It's Not the Shoe Polish

not the shoes
I'm convinced have been with him
since the Second World War

it's not the hands
or their spots
not the way his signature wants to look

it's not the breath the saxophonist takes
early in the record
when he says *look, listen*

it's not the orphanage we visit
or the ancient town
where it sits

it isn't the square of butter
dissolving in the oats
or the way a spoon falls out of focus

it's not the turning over of an engine
or the quiet prayer he says
not the sound of rubber on the cracks he swears to fill

it isn't the hole a hook makes in a thumb
not the sound that wine makes
spilling on a rug

it isn't a ledge
carved where a wedding band once hung
not the red clay accumulated beneath it

not a reflection of empty trees
within it
not the olive not the dove

it's not his name on the spine
on a textbook out of print
not the sound that opening it makes

it isn't Catholic
it's not the Universe
it's not a plot he stakes

in some podunk southern town
it's not a girl across the monkey bars
it's not the way he says her name

it's not the lady at the diner
who wears his accent
like a bit

it's not the eggs not the toast
nor the sum of coffee
that makes a life

it's not the metronome
they implanted
between the margins of his ribs

not the cigar smoke
that encircles
a playground that he built

it has never been a shamrock
the dirty water in the Genesee
or a pair of boxers

left to dry
out on its shore
it's not the mouthfuls of the river

he displaced
not the belly of his beast
it's not the belt he wore on the weekend

not the sound it liked to make
it isn't Christmas
or the lead up to its birth

it's not the names he gave his children
or the curses they entertain
it's all of it, *ĕt Spīritūs Sānctī, Amen*

The Most Sacred Thing in Brooklyn

is a stack of rubber-banded tabs
at the corner bodega

and the yellow tabby cat
that keeps guard

of all of those tallies
of milk and eggs

a pack of cold beer
if it happens to be the weekend

the most hallowed thing in all the borough
is the single look a mother gives

across a makeshift, ancient counter
when she pulls diapers and formula

from above the soda fridge
that says, *I'll get you Friday, Papi*

in a place once named for a skyline
of steeples

the most holy thing around
is the mercy of your corner bodega guy

and his local line of credit
written by hand

and extended whenever a glance
is held a little long

In Puerto Vallarta

where stray chihuahuas walked in pairs
and jungles wept into the sea
and cigarettes came in packs of fourteen
and toro fish, big as your arm
prowled along the shore
and eggs were sold at room temperature
where locals fished the river
and through the flea markets
children ran in ribbons
and fishing skiffs bobbed in the marinas
and iguanas roosted in the palms
and psychedelic flowers
pocked the footpaths
and everywhere, it seemed
that everything
—the abuelas and the damselflies
the grackles and the thunderheads—
looked liked they were dancing

we tried to remember
the kids we were
when we were married
we tried on their nicknames
and their old habits
but we had become ourselves
and so instead, we met them every dawn
and made love from memory
and wondered to ourselves
how our accents
had become intertwined
over the spans of our marriage
like symbiotic trees
or two birds under the same canopy
mimicking each other's song

I Raise Her to Be Free

though she is not
I teach her the definition of it
by the tone of my voice
though she is shackled to my ancestry
I tell her she has a soul
though I'm quite certain
I shouldn't

I give her a name
I hope the wild ether inside
might recognize
and if not
I tell her she is free
to change it
I explain
that we are all
mostly the same
which we are not
I tell her
to look for the typos
in the natural world
so she will recognize them
in her own

I forget the prayers I was made to recite
so we don't have any accidents
when she peels back the veil
I warn her that Abraham
almost stabbed his son
on a dare
I tell her
she has two hearts
but only one recognizes
the sound of my voice
which, I explain
is somewhat reliable
though I know it will abandon her

I implore her to memorize the tone
of a sanctuary
so she will recognize
the discord of its opposite

It's Days Like These

when snow has pulled a curtain
across Manhattan

I pretend that the island
has rowed away

down the East River and up the Hudson
with all of its snares in tow

as law firms in their towers
topple into oyster beds

when museums are forced to return
wandering sarcophagi

to their orphaned homes
when snowflakes

snap like poppers
battering the wake

it's moments
such as these

when the rails hum
when Korean delis

over eggs & cheese
barter with bodegas

and Hoboken
becomes a dream

Brooklyn once had
when the river crested

while tracing with its thumb
a jagged apparition

along a vacant spine
while the northern corridor

has a fire sale with our fountains
aspiring *Appleseeds*

along the freeway
plant shards of Zuccotti Park

commuters maintain
that some trains boomerang

but some tarry into dystopia
where indigenous animals

naturally, have reinstated
an order of mice, who've

chewed through
the breast pockets

of our
formal attire

The Matriarchy Draws a Line

in our daughter's room
inside the Barbie Mansion

where the catch
below the sink

has a leak
and the garage door

has become manual
and the roof is only half-built

and our kid has buried Barbie
out back, in 1950

and knowing her daughter
cannot have it both ways

my wife comes into the living room
with a piece of plastic in her teeth

says, *I think it's time*
to put the Barbie Mansion to bed

half of me wants to finish the roof
the other half considers the work it'd take

to fix the fault that runs the length
of Malibu

The Alphabet Silo!

someone calls
from the field
from behind a mule

first you gotta fill
the alphabet silo
the number silo

the house one
you've got
to put a small plot

in the shadow
of small silos
the arithmetic silo

the money one
and you have to insure it
and you have to name

all of the alphabet babies
someone says
to the woman inside the alphabet house

from the alphabet field
behind the alphabet mule
as he turns

a few
letters over
to see if they glimmer in the ditch

We Sat for Hours

on the parkway
long enough that people were
sitting on their cars
with pizza boxes
in their laps
open-mouthed
like Pac-Mans

she said
this is the first scene
in every dystopian movie

while the title sequence
rolled over the exit ramp and the canopy
boy with dog
lady carrying a brick
tank of oxygen

traveling north
with a week's worth of supplies
we had everything we needed
except clear passage
so we waited
for our turn in the closing credits

girl w/ flashlight under-chin
man of intermittent sorrows
woman holding her shit together
by a single thread

Pathetic Fallacy

as proof that trees
in fact, weep

we submit
for the record

a wheelbarrow
of fallen sky

a foam that follows
newton's eye

a pond of crowns
a pea to loosen

Windsor knots
on golden bedsheets

tied and tossed
out the

second floor
opera door

by kids
raised in a boot

apples dipped
in chloroform

singing swords
breadcrumbs

betwixt
yellow bricks

polygraphs
of wooden boys

a house of sticks
two shakes

of a lamb's tail
three bears

at separate temperatures
four or twenty blackbirds

depending on the recipe
five diamonds in

a bloody mine
sixes, interrogated

to the umpth degree
seven jackpots in a row

over-medicated eights
in a yard of nines

the whole of it, plus
a handful of commandments

standing on our dignity
we submit your honor

these truths as evidence
that we have carved caskets

out of cedar trees
dappled in the divination

of doves, mourning in
acknowledgement that

it's a breeze
to laugh

but, in a tree
it cries

There's This Piano

in my mother's house
that I'm sure is a metaphor

it's probably mahogany
I feel you have to know something private

if you are going to become
its traveler, when afterwards remains

a wooden box of requiems
where underneath, the carpet isn't stained

but all around it, candle wax
grows in vines along its damper

and in the sheet stand, where
once rested a hymnal

a cigarette burns
like a metronome

I feel you'd have to hear *Hail, Mary
Queen of Heaven* played

on its lower register
to understand a hymn

when it's wrapped up like a mourning casserole
where the living sons she originated

can't seem to find their keys
or invite her in the photographs

if I had a daughter,
I'd tell the story

of Nana's piano
like an odyssey

tie an ivory key
around her neck

remove the bridge
hollow out the hull

fortify its ribs
convert it into a bomb shelter

in fact, I *have* a daughter
who Thanksgivings with my mom

in my mind I hold an image
of her at three

banging at the keys
roaring out a sapling yawp

only available to toddlers
and if the piano had a heart

defiance would be its watermark
you could trace a single cord of fury

down to a middle C
a blue vein in the finger of her progeny

these are the particles we make music with
wind chimes, diagonal

in a storm
there is a piano outside my mother's house

not mahogany
but some borderlining color

a mixture of clay and burgundy
and if by accident

you play a *Holy Mary* after her
the *blessed womb* will sound

like a hollowed tree
or the accidental grace

of the fruit
that pushes through its base

You Have to Put the Spoon in Your Mouth

you have to dig in the wreckage
and find blue stones to sew

to your trapped ghost
with the silver thread found between absence and understanding

you have to walk the dish
into a house of grieving mirrors

it's all loose sticks and undergrowth
you'll have to build a shelter from

you have to assume
that only the whole of the forest can survive a thunderstorm

and what falls in it
is your raw materials

you have to work with assumptions
sometimes getting the spoon

to its mouth
will satisfy the belief

that ritual is a part of the accident
whether it's a tragedy, or otherwise

if it's just the spoon and you
you're as redeemable as a stone

the choice is between deferment or departure
the rest is largely parlor tricks

filler for the race to the grave
whatever it is, be it gods or bocce

it isn't made of silver
it doesn't entertain a century

and won't survive its own attention span
the devil doesn't weigh in on mortgage rates

that is how the laws are waged
you trade a lifeboat for a tailgate

you put a tenth of everything
in a basket on the forest's door

and pray you make it to the Super Bowl
or the milestone of your choosing

if it starts with one spoon at daybreak
you hope it ends in coffee cake

or at least that's what you tell the kids
when they graduate from velcro to laces

if nobody told you
you'd be trading one hypocritical horse for another

you've had a cruel faculty
sure, there's the spoon

which assumes getting out of bed
which assumes Lazarus had to be chained to his mattress

for the trick to work
but don't call it what it is

don't look
too far up his sleeves

you still have to dream
to eat

The Moon is From Montana

everybody's heart was once
just a square foot of ideas
we were once
dreamt by drunks

my old man
had a company car
they dug out of a mountain
with shovels made
from the spare parts
of a Buick

there's a set of tracks
below the riverbed
where no train has ever run
about which I'd like
to write a book comprised
of only parting words

for every car crash on the highway
there's a rosary bead
sparking in my grandmother's pocket
she pats when she's nervous
her children haven't called
the last pope wrote a letter
my grandfather put in a frame
and when he died
I took it down
to trace the Roman numbers

the moon is Midwestern
it makes better conversation
with the grains than I
it bribes the tides for summer storms
and when it doesn't rain
it thunders
in between the lightning strikes

coming off a string of relics
and spare parts found
deep inside a mountain

One of the Most Beautiful Things

I have ever seen
is a rain soaked train
roll into the station
is a halo of chalky footprints
around a day-old hopscotch court
is a child
drawing out her plans
for a costume
in secret
in her room
a few weeks before
Halloween
is someone holding her breath
underwater on film
or through a tunnel
a couple drunks
sharing a newspaper
for shelter
is a vine
choking the name
on a wicked man's grave
is my old man
folding a napkin
around his spoon

I don't think living is easy
most days I cannot bear
to watch a person
call to mind
the way she likes her coffee
I like to guess the weights of a heavy clouds
to understand their troubles
on a good day
a group of laughing men
in bowling uniforms
can send me into stitches
but ordinarily, it just
reduces me to tears

I Have No Time for the Poets

who declare this emerging era
with no sense of accountability

as if the borders will melt
in the rain

and the tanks
will remove their own rivets

and a woman in a hijab
simply wandering down the sidewalk

will forget to check her peripheries
in a neighborhood she's never traversed

if this time is ours
men will have to be struck

after *all*
and before

are created equal
and replaced with creatures

and we'll have to do away
with creation

we will have to accept our place
in the spilling evolution

before we abandon our properties
before we begin to share the squares again

before squares can return to us
meandering

before the winds
can pass through the tall grasses

and the coal can be left
inside the belly of a mountain

someone will have to pull a brick
from our southern wall

and pass a note through
to her neighbor

somebody will have to shred the flags
and sew the strips together

we will have to blend the stars
with the union jacks

we will have to declare
our independence from old declarations

if we are to make new ones
if we are to accept ourselves

amongst equal creatures
somebody will have to curse the golden altars

someone else will have to walk an elder god
from the church to the temple

I have no time for infancy of thought
when it comes to the emerging world

I haven't a second of breath
to waste on the waiters

I know the seeds
are eventual

I know the bees
deserve equal opportunity

but I have hands for sowing
I have been handed

the knowledge that accompanies
my right to ancestry

my coat is lined
with surrender flags

its leather was once
the binding of a Bible

my buttons are made from rivets
that once held together wars

Should You Meet Me on Your Way Home to Rochester

because your son resembles us
should you stop
and name the children in his boot

if the hunting posts
have taken on the weather in your head
if the skies
full of birds
are relative
to a painting
in your mother's favorite room
if the cans are full
with the same amount of shot

should you stop and see a report
on an antiquated TV
about a harangued field goal
or a riot that crossed the Genesee

should the Kodak mountains
fan across Highway 86
like a table spread
or fingers on an organ's keys

remember how many Rochesters
how many cans of shot
are piled up in the allegories
know you aren't the man they stole
with darkroom chemicals, that is
should you ever catch sight of me
on your way home to another Rochester
of a different name

Notes

Epigraph for Ch. 1: *Pinocchio*; Carlo Collodi, 1881

"I Began to Wonder" & "On Second Thought" are based on Joanna Solfrian's *"Three Joannas and I Was Not One"*; 2019

Epigraph for "The Devil and Robert Johnson" is from physicist Eugene Wigner's *Symmetries and Reflections*; 1979

Epigraph for Ch 2. is from Denver Butson's poem "Weariness": 2020

"On Not Seeing the Red Bird Off the Coast of Argentina" and "More Than Ever" are based on Iris Dunkle's poem "On Seeing the Red Bird Off the Coast of Argentina"; 2019

Terence Degnan is the author of three books of poetry, including *I Can Wonder Anything* (Finishing Line, 2023). His work has appeared widely in anthologies and literary journals. His spoken word album, *BC*, was adapted for the stage in New York City, where he lives with his wife, Melanie, and daughter, Lola, who came up with the title of his newest book.

www.ingramcontent.com/pod-product-compliance
Lightning Source LLC
Chambersburg PA
CBHW030222170426
43194CB00007BA/833